OTHER BOOKS BY
CAROLINE THOMAS HARNSBERGER

Mark Twain at Your Fingertips, 1948
The Lincoln Treasury, 1950
A Man of Courage, Robert A. Taft, 1952
Mark Twain, Family Man, 1960

MARK TWAIN'S
VIEWS OF RELIGION

Mark Twain in London, 1899

Mark Twain's
VIEWS OF RELIGION

by

Caroline Thomas Harnsberger

THE SCHORI PRESS · EVANSTON, ILLINOIS

1961

Acknowledgements

APPRECIATION is here expressed to Clara Clemens Samossoud and the Trustees of the Estate of Samuel L. Clemens for permission to quote heretofore unpublished Twain material.

Also, grateful acknowledgment is made to Harper & Brothers for permission to quote from the following works:

My Father, Mark Twain Clara Clemens, copyright 1931.
Mark Twain in Eruption ed. Bernard De Voto, copy. 1940.
My Mark Twain William Dean Howells, copy. 1910.
Mark Twain's Autobiography ed. Albert Bigelow Paine, copy. 1924.
Mark Twain's Letters ed. Albert Bigelow Paine, copy. 1917.
Mark Twain's Notebook ed. Albert Bigelow Paine, copy. 1935.
Christian Science Mark Twain, copy. 1899.
A Connecticut Yankee Mark Twain, copy. 1899.
Europe & Elsewhere Mark Twain, copy. 1923.
Huckleberry Finn Mark Twain, copy. 1899.
The Innocents Abroad Mark Twain, copy. 1899.
Literary Essays Mark Twain, copy. 1899.
Puddn'head Wilson Mark Twain, copy. 1899.
Mark Twain's Speeches ed. Albert Bigelow Paine, copy. 1910.
Roughing It Mark Twain, copy. 1899.
A Tramp Abroad Mark Twain, copy. 1899.
The Love Letters of Mark Twain ed. Dixon Wecter, copy. 1949.

To Alfred A. Knopf, for *Mark Twain's Travels with Mr. Brown* ed. Franklin Walker and G. Ezra Dane, copy. 1940; to George Fields, *The Washoe Giant in San Francisco*, ed. Franklin Walker, copy. 1938; to Harvard University Press, *Mark Twain-Howells Letters*, Henry Nash Smith & William M. Gibson, copy. 1960; to the Viking Press, *The Portable Mark Twain*, ed. Bernard De Voto, copy. 1946; to Columbia University Press, *Mark Twain's Letters to Mary*, ed. Lewis Leary, copy. 1961; to Oklahoma University Press, *Mark Twain, the Man and His Work*, 1961.

Preface

MARK TWAIN was an enthusiastic reader of a variety of classical and contemporary books, including biographies, histories, memoirs, science and theology. He showed his agreements or disagreements with the authors by inscribing notes in the margins throughout their works. His opinions, usually written in pencil, were more characteristically frank because he intended them to be for his own amusement and future reference and not for publication. The comments were often entertaining and revealing.

Where, for instance, could one find a more concise opinion of statesmanship than in Twain's six-word notation: "Statesmanship and assmanship are spelt different"?[1]

Occasionally his habit back-fired. After reading a biography of Daniel Boone by Abbott, he wrote on the fly-leaf: "A poor slovenly book, a mess of sappy drivel, and bad grammar."

His nine-year-old daughter, Clara, was charmed with the observation without understanding it, and carried the book away to read. "It must be lovely," she said.

When Twain found a book controversial in nature, like Jonathan Edwards' *Freedom of the Will*, or Rufus K. Noyes' *Views of Religion*, he literally filled its margins with ideas and rebuttals. In a theological treatise, this kind of comment often appeared:

"Gods have always been born out of wedlock—apparently there is no other way to make them respectable."[2]

Noyes' book, a compilation of thousands of unorthodox religious opinions written by prominent persons of the Nineteenth Century, was presented to the 71-year-old Twain by Noyes in 1906, with the inscription:

"Until ethics changes its name or religion its character, keep them independent and separate; as they are essentially unlike."

Mark Twain did not agree with every doctrine expressed in the volume. His extensive marginal notes, printed here for the first time, are the inspiration for this resumé of his views of religion.

CAROLINE THOMAS HARNSBERGER

Mark Twain's Views of Religion

Those who are unacquainted with the transcendental leaning of Mark Twain are inclined to dismiss him as an atheist. Because he was a freethinker he could not be fit into a church creed or any of the usual religious patterns, (as he put it, he was not "a very dusty Christian"), but his preoccupation with God as a Supreme Being proved him to be far from an atheist.

He expressed an absorbing interest in religion and tried to define it. To him it appeared to "consist of a set of things which the average man thinks he believes and wishes he was certain."[3] In a still less conforming moment he wrote: "The cat's tail is only an incumbrance to her, yet she thinks it is the most precious thing she has got. Just so with man and his religion." [4] Yet, he had his own, and it was probably as simple as that described by Huck Finn:

"I think't if a feller he'ps another feller when he's in trouble, and don't cuss, and don't do no mean things, nur noth'n he ain' no business to do, and don't spell the Saviour's name with a little g, he ain't runnin' no resks,— he's about as saift as if he b'longed to a church." [5]

The subject of religion is ever-present in Twain's writing; in his standard works alone there are 125 allusions to the Bible, besides many concepts expressed in his notebooks and letters.

When he dissented from the "unjust, pitiless God" pictured in the Old Testament, or when he complained:

"What God lacks is convictions—stability of character. He ought to be a Presbyterian or a Catholic or *something*—not try to be everything," [6] he was referring to the Biblical God and objecting to the depiction because he considered the Book to be entirely the work of man, not inspired by God. "The problem of life and death and eternity and the true conception of God is a bigger thing than is contained in that book." [7] The belief prompted him to write further: "I think we are only the microscopic trichina concealed in the blood of some vast creature's veins, and that it is that vast creature whom God concerns himself about and not us." [8]

Since these attacks on the scriptural God appear irreverent to orthodox believers, Twain must again be explained on his own terms: "I can go as far as the next

2

man in genuine reverence of holy things," he said, "but stretching the narrow garment of belief to fit the broad shoulders of a wish, 'tis too much for me."[9]

He continued: "I was never consciously and purposely irreverent in my life, yet one person or another is always charging me with a lack of reverence. Reverence for what—for whom? Who is to decide what ought to command my reverence—my neighbor or I? I think I ought to do the electing myself. The Mohammedan reveres Mohammed—it is his privilege; the Christian doesn't—apparently that is his privilege; the account is square enough. They haven't any right to complain of the other, yet they do complain of each other, and that is where the unfairness comes in. Each says that the other is irreverent, and both are mistaken, for manifestly you can't have reverence for a thing that doesn't command it. If you could do that you could digest what you haven't eaten, and do other miracles and get a reputation."[10]

Whatever skeptical views he aired, and he became increasingly skeptical as he grew older, the changes in his attitude contradicted what he termed "a but-little considered fact in human nature: that the religious folly you are born in you will *die* in, no matter what apparently reasonabler religious folly may seem to have taken its place meanwhile and abolished and obliterated it."[11] It is difficult to find a precise point in Twain's life where his posture toward religion changed. But we can at least survey his background of religious exposures to determine the factors which produced the evolution of his religious thought and influenced him most toward becoming an apostate.

THE SMALL boy, Samuel Clemens, was raised in Hannibal, Missouri, a Mississippi River town which, in 1847—twelve years after his birth—boasted a population of 2500 and six organized congregations. The Presbyterian Church had been the first to build a house of worship, and as early as 1840, Mrs. Clemens had become a member and taken her children with her to the services. Here in the Sunday School Sam and his brothers and sister were drilled in the catechism and the mysteries of Calvinism.

It was not an easy faith to learn; much of it, including damnation, hell-fire and brimstone, could not be explained, but it sank deep into the sensitive nature of Sam and developed in him "a trained Presbyterian conscience, which knew but one duty . . . to hunt and harry its slave on all pretexts—particularly when there was no sense or reason to it."[12] Twain was to make a similar comment later in *Huck Finn*, through Huck himself: "It don't make no difference whether you do right or wrong, a person's conscience goes for him *anyway*. If I had a yaller dog that didn't know any more than a person's conscience does I would pisen him. It takes up more room than all the rest

4

of a person's insides, and yet ain't no good, nohow."[13] In *A Connecticut Yankee*, he concluded: "If I had the remaking of man, he wouldn't have any conscience...I have noticed my conscience for many years, and I know it is more trouble and bother to me than anything else I started with. I suppose that in the beginning I prized it, because we prize anything that is ours; and yet how foolish it was to think so. If we look at it in another way, we see how absurd it is: if I had an anvil in me would I prize it? Of course not. And yet when you come to think, there is no real difference between a conscience and an anvil — I mean for comfort... You could dissolve an anvil with acids, when you couldn't stand it any longer; but there isn't any way that you can work off a conscience—at least so it will stay worked off; not that I know of, anyway."[14]

Sam's faith in Sunday School teachings was not strengthened by the outcome of the expulsion from his class of an unruly boy. Later, when the lad disappeared from Hannibal, it became a rumor—whispered with awe from boy to boy—that the Devil had carried him off. But one day a steamboat docked at the Hannibal wharf, and from it stepped the one the Devil was supposed to have taken, resplendent in the blue uniform and gold buttons of a cabin boy.

Sam was required to continue his dutiful attendance at church school, to recite verses from the Bible, and to endure the confinement as best he could, but he learned most "to fear God and dread the Sunday School." He was taught to keep the Sabbath, as well, however difficult it became for his mother to enforce it. He said later: "We didn't break the Sabbath often enough to signify— once a week perhaps. But we were good boys, good Presbyterian boys...anyway, we were good Presbyterian boys when the weather was doubtful; when it was fair, we did wander a little away from the fold."[15] Another comment, made in his old age: "God runs his worldly business just the same on Sunday as he does on week-days, but if you and I break the Sabbath we get damned for it."[16] One time he devised a plan to overcome the Sunday restrictions against playing games—"to name the chess men after some of the old Bible heroes and then play chess on Sunday."[17]

Any wrong committed by the mischievous Sam was "righted" through his attending a second church service with his mother on Sunday evening. It was punishment to be endured but lacking as an inspiration toward reform. After all his mother's effort, there was only one thing that could bring the boy to terms—a thunderstorm. The fearsome darkness, the lightning flashes and the loud thunder were to him the voice of God speaking through his conscience and impelling him to pray to lead a better life and go to Sunday School the following Sabbath without objection. Regarding lightning, he once wrote a marginal note: "God's lightning strikes more churches than any other property."[18]

6

Alongside his orthodox schooling Sam was no doubt influenced by his father, an admirer of Thomas Jefferson and a follower of Jefferson's skepticism. Mr. Clemens was a respected member of the community, but he did not set before his children the example of his own church-going. After his death, when Sam was only twelve, Mrs. Clemens continued to expose her offspring to that mainstay of good Presbyterian teaching, the rigid Westminster catechism. She saw to it that they were taught God Almighty had made the world for His glory and that men were but clay in His hands. God's omnipotent will was the source of all that happened, and He willed not only the pleasant things, but the unpleasant—earthquakes, wars, epidemics, accidents, drownings, etc., and by His sovereign decree some souls went to heaven and others to eternal damnation. But it was also from his mother and her sense of humor that Sam learned the lesson of tolerance. ("Intolerance is everything for oneself, and nothing for the other person.") [19] Later, he would write:

"I am quite sure I have no race prejudices, and I think I have no color prejudices nor caste prejudices nor creed prejudices. All I care to know is that a man is a human being—that is enough for me; he can't be any worse. I have no special regard for Satan; but I can at least claim that I have no prejudice against him. It may even be that I lean a little his way, on account of his not having a fair show. All religions issue bibles against him, and say the most injurious things about him, but we never hear *his* side. We have none but the evidence for the prosecution, and yet we have rendered the verdict. To my mind, this is irregular...Of course Satan has some kind of a case, it goes without saying. It may be a poor one, but that is nothing; that can be said about any of us ... We may not pay him reverence, for that would be indiscreet, but we can at least respect his talents. A person who has for untold centuries maintained the imposing position of spiritual head of four-fifths of the human race, and political head of the whole of it, must be granted the possession of executive abilities of the loftiest order. In his large presence the other popes and politicians shrink to midges for the microscope. I would like to see him. I would rather see him and shake him by the tail than any other member of the European Concert." [20]

Though apparently strict in the religious training of her children, Mrs. Clemens was no martyr to her beliefs. When inconsistency between her theories and practice was pointed out, she replied:

"Religion is a jugfull; I hold a dipperfull. I know a person that can turn his cheek is higher and holier than I am...but I despise him, too, and wouldn't have him for a doormat." [21]

8

THE citizens of Hannibal, like their Puritan ancestors, were a conscientious people, willing for the Church to sway them to a deeper consciousness of sin and the need for repentance. The Church warned of the divine wrath to be visited upon sinners and pointed out the coming of the Judgment Day. Twain recalled later that Hannibal had but one avowed "unbeliever," a young Kentucky lawyer, "a fascinating cuss." Profane and blasphemous, he was vain of being prayed for in the revivals, and of the young ladies' desire to convert him. The villagers "believed the devil would come for him in person some stormy night." [22]

An active institution of influence in the town was The Cadets of Temperance—an anti-alcoholic, anti-tobacco and anti-profanity organization which crusaded by means of parades and revivals. It attracted Sam because he thought he never could be truly happy until he wore one of those stunning red scarfs and walked in procession when a distinguished citizen died. "I stood it four months," he said, "but never an infernal distinguished citizen died during the whole time; and when they finally pronounced old Dr. Norton convalescent (a man I had been depending on for seven or eight weeks), I just drew out. I drew out in disgust, and pretty much all the distinguished citizens in the camp died within the next three weeks."[23]

On the temperance subject, Twain wrote in his Notebook: "Temperate temperance is best. Intemperate temperance injures the cause of temperance, while temperate temperance helps it in its fight against intemperate intemperance. Fanatics will never learn that though it be written in letters of gold across the sky."[24]

The Campbellite sect, or Disciples of Christ, headed by Alexander Campbell, was also on the march, and held camp meetings in Hannibal. Sam, then an apprentice printer, had occasion to set some of Campbell's sermons in type, as well as to hear the great evangelist during the revivals. His satire on religious emotionalism written later in *Huck Finn* leaves no doubt that he had attended camp meetings.

In addition to the churches' emphasis on fear and the villagers' admonitions that every tragedy and storm was the work of a God of vengeance, Sam was associated with Negro servants whose superstitions about "ha'nts" and omens of death served to deepen the impressionable boy's sense of guilt and his fear of dying lost and tormented for not being converted. The God Sam learned about from the Negroes probably frightened him more than the God preached about in his church because "de Lawd" of the colored man reached down where he lived.

ANOTHER influence in the life of Sam Clemens was his uncle John Quarles, a freethinker, at whose home in Missouri the boy spent several summers. The newest discoveries of geologists and astronomers interested Quarles, and had he lived to hear Darwin's theory of evolution, supported by Thomas Huxley, no doubt he would have relished those views and upheld them against the Bible's account of the origin of man.

Before he was fifteen, Sam was required to read the Bible from cover to cover — a stint commonly inflicted by parents of that day upon their children. He wrote later:

"All indecent books are forbidden by law, except the Bible. Yet it corrupts more young people than all the others put together. For 400 years the Bible has been soiling the minds of Protestant children of both sexes. No individual of them has ever escaped. They have all reveled in the salacious passages secretly.

"Three of our libraries have thrown *Huck Finn* out as being an unclean book. Next they will be wanting an expurgated Bible." [25]

In spite of this, Sam's interest in the Bible continued. Although he still felt as he grew older that "one who reads an unexpurgated Bible can never draw a clean, sweet breath again this side of the grave," he began to appreciate the literary quality of the Book. At the age of thirty-two, he read it through once more before taking a trip to the Holy Land in 1867. Then he wrote:

"It is hard to make a choice of the most beautiful passage in a book which is so gemmed with beautiful passages as the Bible, but it is certain that not many things within its lids may take rank above the exquisite story of Joseph. Who taught those ancient writers their simplicity of language, their felicity of expression, their pathos, and, above all, their faculty of sinking themselves entirely out of sight of the reader and making the narrative stand out alone and seem to tell itself? Shakespeare is always present when one reads his book; Macaulay is present when we follow the march of his stately sentences; but the Old Testament writers are hidden from view."[26]

Perhaps something of the simplicity of the King James version crept into his own style; certainly he fell naturally into such Biblical expressions as "be content and praise God"; "there was wailing and gnashing of teeth", and "you have clothed her in garments for her high degree." Charles Warren Stoddard, one of Twain's secretaries, described an occasion when "the humorist read the Book of Ruth with tears in his voice and some verses from Isaiah in a style that would have melted the hardest heart."

During a stay in San Francisco in 1865, Twain was influenced by the father of William Randolph Hearst to become independent in his political and religious thinking. He wrote in 1906:

"I have never belonged to any party from that day to

this. I have never belonged to any church from that day to this. I have remained absolutely free in those matters. And in this independence I have found a spiritual comfort and a peace of mind quite above price." [26a] In 1865, also, he began to object to conventional set prayers.

In 1870, Sam Clemens was married to Olivia Langdon, daughter of a wealthy family in Elmira, New York, and a member of the Park Congregational Church led by Thomas K. Beecher. This minister, like his sister, Harriet Beecher Stowe, and his brother, Henry Ward Beecher, was a creative thinker who plead for religious tolerance and rejected cut and dried sectarianism in an attempt to reconcile religion with the latest findings in science. Regarding this endeavor, Twain commented: "When religion and science elect to live together, it is a plain case of adultery." [27] In their pulpits neither Thomas nor Henry Ward Beecher yielded to theological hair-splitting, but concentrated their preaching on the Fatherhood of God and the Brotherhood of man. The broad point of view was held also by Mrs. Thomas Beecher, who in turn transmitted it to Olivia Langdon in her Sunday School class.

Thus Olivia's background provided her with a flexibility to live more easily with a man who had begun to chafe against formal religion, and who finally became a complete skeptic. For some months she was able to persuade her husband to say grace before meals and to read a chapter of the Bible each morning. When she realized that his logical mind refused to accept the Bible as a guide to spiritual salvation, that it was to him merely a mass of fables and traditions—a kind of mythology, she too gave up the ceremony. Clemens's growing awareness that humanity had built its highest hope, the doctrines of its faith on material in the Bible caused him to explode:

"Livy, you may keep this up if you want to, but I must ask you to excuse me from it. It is making me a hypocrite. I don't believe in this Bible. It contradicts my reason. I can't sit here and listen to it, letting you believe that I regard it, as you do, in the light of gospel, the word of God." [28]

In a letter written shortly before their engagement Clemens had warned Olivia that he was even then wavering in his religious faith:

"I thank you for all you say about religion, Livy, and I have as much confidence as yourself that I shall succeed at last, but Oh, it is slow and often discouraging. I am happy in conducting myself rightly—but the emotion, the revealing religious emotion, Livy, *will not* come, it seems to me. I pray for it—it is all I can do. I know not how to compel an emotion. And I pray every day that you may not be impatient or lose confidence in my final conversion. I pray that you may keep your courage and be of good heart. And I pray that my poisonous and besetting *apathy* may pass from me. It is hard to be a Christian *in spirit*, Livy, though the mere letter of the law seems not very difficult as a general thing. I have hope." [29]

For a year or two after Clemens installed his family in Hartford, Connecticut, (October 1871) he continued to please his wife by attending the services of the Asylum Hill Congregational Church, ministered by their close friend, Joseph H. Twichell. "It 'most kills me, but I go," he told William Dean Howells. Presently, they both ceased attending church regularly, Livy saying to her husband, "Well, if you are to be lost, I want to be lost with you." [30] Many years afterward, the Clemens's only surviving daughter, Clara, minimized her mother's remark as being suitable to a particular mood and not to be taken too seriously. "I think that anyone with so deep a faith as Mother's could hardly lose it absolutely," but she agreed that "living with someone who voiced the opposite feelings so long would certainly take the edge off its beauty and warmth." And she added: "I personally do not see how anyone lives a day without God." [31]

It is certain that during crises in her life, particularly bereavements, Olivia turned to God with her prayers, yet, when her husband once said to her: "Livy, if it comforts you to lean on the Christian faith, do so," she answered, "I can't, Youth. I haven't any." [32] She had retreated from orthodoxy.

Nearly two years after her marriage, Livy wrote her husband: "Mother and I went to church this morning.... It is so long since I have been to church that I was mellowed by the very atmosphere I think, Mr. Twichell's prayer touched me, and made me cry. He prayed particularly for those who had fallen away and were longing to come back to God. Youth, I am ashamed to go back, because I have fallen away so many times and gone back feeling that if I ever should grow cold again, it would be useless trying, because I never could have more earnest and prayerful and even at times heart broken determination to keep by the truth and the right and strive for God's spirit—it would seem if I did not remain steadfast after such times, I never could...How I do want you at home Darling...you are a dear little man—I am grateful that my heart is so filled with love for you. Mrs. Warner was speaking this P.M. of lukewarmness toward God. She said she used to be greatly troubled about it, but lately she thinks that is of no consequence, our moods are different, we do not always feel alike toward our husbands—I told her if I felt toward God as I did toward my husband I should never be in the least troubled—I did not tell her how almost perfectly cold I am toward God." [33]

A month later she wrote another disturbed letter:

"This morning...Mr. Twichell gave us a *very good* sermon....When I went in and saw that it was the communion service, my heart sank because I do feel so unfit to go to the table of communion, yet cannot bear to go away from it. Mr. Twichell gave such an *earnest* invitation to all those who were feeling cold and far away from God and discouraged to stay and get comfort, that I could not come away. I staid and of course my prayers were for you and myself...." [34]

Clemens's conscience was always weighed down with his

influence upon his wife, and after her death he moaned:

"I took Livy's religion away from her, and gave her nothing—worse than nothing—in return. I gave her alarm." [35]

He wrote Clara: "I recognize with the deepest satisfaction that you are safe in the spiritual shelter and refuge which all women and most men need, and I hope I shall be spared the crime of violating its sanctities and impairing its solaces and comforts as I did in your mother's case—almost the only crime of my life which causes me bitterness now. (I must not dwell upon this subject.)..." [36]

Twain's tolerance of other religions was proved when he welcomed into his family a Jew, the highly-respected musician, Gabrilowitsch, whom Clara married in 1909.

IT IS curious that Twain's unorthodox views were not moderated by the numerous ministers with whom he made friends through the years, although it must be admitted that he associated with those of wider belief than the average pastor of his day. Among them were Joshua P. Tucker, Presbyterian in Hannibal; Franklin B. Rising, Episcopalian in Virginia City, Nevada; Horatio Stebbins, Unitarian in San Francisco; Thomas K. Beecher, Congregationalist, in Elmira, N.Y.; Horace Bushnell, Congregationalist and early dissenter against Calvinism, in Hartford, and his closest friend, Joseph H. Twichell.

17

Twain spent many hours with Twichell in both his own home and Twichell's, on walking tours around Hartford and in Europe on tramps in the Alps. While the author was living with his family in Europe for several years he maintained a correspondence with Twichell and jokingly mentioned the "pew-rent" he was saving by living abroad. It was during one of their endless discussions, in 1878, that Twain burst out:

"Joe, I'm going to make a confession. I don't believe in your religion at all . . . I've been living a lie right straight along whenever I pretended to. For a moment, sometimes, I have been almost a believer, but it immediately drifts away from me again. I don't believe one word of your Bible was inspired by God any more than any other book. I believe it is entirely the work of man from beginning to end—atonement and all . . ." [37]

The personal side of religious discussion thereupon closed between them, never to be reopened. Twichell, as had other clergymen before him, recognized in Twain a seeker of Truth and regarded his occasional eruptions of profanity and excessive smoking as only surface blemishes on a character of sterling worth. Some suspected that his religious life was disturbed by the fact that he simply had a good share of rebel in him. One scholar found it astonishing that this never took the form of moral rebellion: "This shows what a *good* man he really was. His rebellion, too, was connected with many of his finest qualities; it enabled him to look straight through many of the hideous evils of his time by which most of the good 'Christians' were taken in." [38]

It has never been satisfactorily explained—even by Clara Clemens herself, why the three Clemens daughters were never sent to Sunday School. Susy, at five, once told a visitor that she "had been in a church only once and that was the day that Clara was crucified."[christened]. There was a practical reason, that they could not be taken to the church because Mrs. Clemens liked to give Patrick, the coachman, a complete day of rest, on Sunday, but there was the more likely reason that Olivia wished to superimpose upon her children her own interpretations of the Bible and her own methods of directing their thoughts toward God. The girls themselves preferred to stay home as a matter of habit, since they received all their other schooling at home under private tutors and enjoyed their life as it was.

The subject of Biblical interpretation always furnished Twain a jumping off place into his own theories. In the 1870s he was moved to write on the human idea of God, ancient and modern:

"The difference in importance, between the God of the Bible and the God of the present day, cannot be described, it can only be vaguely and inadequately figured to the mind . . . If you make figures to represent the earth and moon, and allow a space of one inch between them, to represent the 400,000 miles of distance which lies between the two bodies, the map will have to be

19

1,100 miles long in order to bring in the nearest fixed star. So one cannot put the modern heavens on a map, nor the modern God; but the Bible God and the Bible heavens can be set down on a slate and yet not be discommoded . . .

"The difference between that universe and the modern one revealed by science is as the difference between a dust-flecked ray in a barn and the sublime arch of the Milky Way in the skies. Its God was strictly proportioned to its dimensions. His sole solicitude was about a handful of truculent nomads. He worried and fretted over them in a peculiarly and distractingly human way. One day he coaxed and petted them beyond their deserts. He sulked, he cursed, he raged, he grieved, according to his mood and the circumstances, but all to no purpose; his efforts were all vain, he could not govern them. When the fury was on him he was blind to all reason—he not only slaughtered the offender, but even his harmless little children and dumb cattle . . .

"To trust the God of the Bible is to trust an irascible, vindictive, fierce and ever fickle and changeful master; to trust the true God is to trust a Being who has uttered no promises, but whose beneficent, exact, and changeless ordering of the machinery of his colossal universe is proof that He is at least steadfast to His purposes; whose unwritten laws, so far as they affect man, being equal and impartial, show that He is just and fair; these things, taken together, suggest that if He shall ordain us to live hereafter, He will still be steadfast, just and fair toward us. We shall not need to require anything more." [39]

Twain's travels through numerous foreign countries, including India and Africa, enabled him to observe the creeds and customs of other religions and to compare them with Christianity, not entirely to their disadvantage. He wrote:

"The wise Fiji chief said to a missionary: 'We do not pray to the Good Spirit to spare us, but to the other one; a *good* spirit is not going to hurt us.'" [40]

"I bring you the stately matron named Christendom, returning bedraggled, besmirched and dishonored from pirate raids upon the helpless Filipinos, the Boers, the Chinese, the Hereros, etc., with her soul full of meanness, her pocket full of boodle and her mouth full of pious hypocrisies." [41]

"Would it not be prudent to get our civilization tools together in the way of glass beads and theology, Maxim guns and hymn books?" [42]

"The entire Christian religion came from older (but probably not 'grosser') religions. It is quite sufficiently gross, in morals, facts, and language." [43]

21

Among his frequent references to Christianity, Twain clarified his position: "Neither Howells nor I believe in hell or the divinity of the Savior, but no matter, the Savior is none the less a sacred Personage, and a man should have no desire or disposition to refer to him lightly, profanely, or otherwise than with the profoundest reverence."[44]

And he stated in 1871: "All that is great and good in our civilization came from the hand of Jesus." [44a]

When someone mentioned that this is a Christian country, he replied: "Why...so is hell. Inasmuch as 'Strait is the way and narrow is the gate, and few—*few*—are they that enter in thereat' has had the natural effect of making hell the only really prominent Christian community in any of the worlds; but we don't brag of this and certainly it is not proper to boast that America is a Christian country when we all know that five-sixths of our population could not enter in at the narrow gate."[45]

He quoted a Bishop from China who said: "Four fifths of the human race know not God. God can't do all the work; we must help." [45a]

As he observed, Christians did not behave well. In the midst of a wave of lynchings in this country in 1901, he wrote: "O kind missionary, O compassionate missionary, leave China! come home and convert these Christians!" [46]

"Since the beginning of the world there have been 225 billion savages born and damned and 28,000 saved by missionary effort." [47]

In 1866, he noted in Hawaii that there are "more

22

missionaries and more row made about saving these 60,000 people than it would take to convert hell itself." [48] "How sad it is to think of the multitudes who have gone to their graves in this beautiful island and never knew there was a hell." [49]

As for me, I hope to be cremated. I made that remark to my pastor once, who said, with what he thought was an impressive manner, "I wouldn't worry about that if I had your chances." Much he knew about it—the family all so opposed to it.

from Life on the Mississippi, *first issue, p. 441*

23

"You can't write up hell so it will stand printing," he commented, but added: "Heaven for climate; Hell for society." [50]

Twain wrote *Captain Stormfield's Visit to Heaven* as a satire on the pettiness of sectarians. He jotted in his notes:

"Man's heaven is a place of reward—of previous delights—made it himself, mind you—all out of his own head. Very well; of the delights of *this* world man cares *most* for sexual intercourse. He will. . .risk fortune, character, reputation, life itself. And what. . .has he done? . . .you would never guess—*he has left it out of his heaven!* Prayer takes its place." [51]

RETURNING to the Bible, he said:

"There is a curious poverty of invention in Bibles. Most of the great races each have one, and they all show this striking defect: each pretends to originality, without possessing any. Each of them borrows from the other, confiscates old stage properties, puts them forth as fresh and new inspirations from on high. We borrowed the Golden Rule from Confucius, after it had seen service for centuries, and copyrighted it without a blush." [52] He added: "The Golden Rule was a million years old before Confucius was born. It is a natural maxim." [53]

"Incidentally, the Golden Rule was made of hard

24

metal so it could stand severe wear, it not being known at that time that butter would answer." [54]

"Yes, the Golden Rule exists, it continues to sparkle, and it is well taken care of. It is exhibit A in the Church's assets, and we pull it out every Sunday and give it an airing...It is strictly religious furniture, like an acolyte, or a contribution-plate, or any of those things, but it is not intruded into business." [55]

. . .

"In the Bible we went back to Babylon for the Deluge, and we are as proud of it and as satisfied with it as if it had been worth the trouble; whereas we know now that Noah's flood never happened, and couldn't have happened—not in that way. The flood is a favorite with Bible-makers. Another favorite with the founders of religions is the Immaculate Conception. It had been worn threadbare; but we adopted it as a new idea. It was old in Egypt several thousand years before Christ was born. The Hindus prized it ages ago. The Egyptians adopted it even for some of their kings. The Romans borrowed the idea from Greece. We got it straight from heaven by way of Rome. We are still charmed with it." [56]

. . .

That Mark Twain was hazy in his understanding of the Immaculate Conception and the Virgin Birth is evidenced in some of his marginal notes:

"Might an elephant, enjoying improper...relations with a microbe, do the immaculate conception stunt?"

25

In a Notebook, he commented:

"The Immaculate Conception could not be repeated successfully in New York in our day. It would produce laughter, not reverence and adoration." [57]

. . .

"When we reflect upon the origins of Krishna, Buddha, Christ and the others we are struck with the fact that virgins are not as fertile now as they used to be."

"Fertile virgins—like miracles—have gone out."

. . .

"Christian Science must inevitably fail, unless Mrs. Eddy can prove that she was born of a virgin."

. . .

"If it should turn out that a Chicago virgin has given birth to God Almighty, would Chicago believe it? Even on the testimony of shepherds and cowboys?" [58]

. . .

Clara Clemens said she saw tears come often to the eyes of her father when great beauty and his adoration of nature overwhelmed him. She knew that he believed in a creative God, that his God was a larger God beyond all narrow tenets and creeds. His God was a great Mind which exerts its care of the individual through the immutable laws of time and change and enviroment—the Supreme God which comprehends the individual plant, animal or human being only as a unit in a bigger scheme of life and love. Again he was merely objecting to the small human conception of the Supreme Being.

This was evident in one of his Notebooks, written in 1905, when Alfred Wallace, the astronomer, announced the universe was made for man. Twain wrote:

"Mr. Wallace has proved that the universe was made for this world, and that this world was made for man. There being 22 billion microbes in each man, and feeding upon him, we now perceive who the whole outfit was made for." [59]

In the margins of another book in his library, he wrote:

"Man was on earth 200,000 years before God remembered whom it was He built coal for.

"It is a marvel that He didn't think of providing pumps—and capital." [60]

. . .

Inside the cover of the book *Sketches of Creation* (1903), he wrote:

"It was a time when grown-up children were still trying to mix fact and fiction: Geology and Theology."

"Theology seems to be an ass." [61]

. . .

As to Creation, Twain expressed a typical opinion:

"It has the look of a child amusing itself: it makes a shell-fish and sea-weed for ten million years, then tires of them and destroys them; makes fishes for ten million years, then tires of them and destroys them; makes stupendous vegetation for ten million years, populating it with prodigious reptiles—tires of them and destroys them: makes mammals of a queer sort for ten million years—

27

tires of them and destroys them. Then for 10,000 years it makes Man. By all the laws of logical deduction, *his* fate is easy to foresee.

"And all these aeons and aeons of trivial fussing in order that we might have [Teddy] Roosevelt! The dignity of God is established." [62]

. . .

"If man would only trust in Him who doeth all things well and keep his bowels open, every little thing wouldn't scare him so." [63]

. . .

Approaching the age of fifty, Twain wrote:

"The suns and planets that form the constellations of a billion billion solar systems and go pouring, a tossing flood of shining globes, through the viewless arteries of space are the blood-corpuscles in the veins of God; and the nations are the microbes that swarm and wiggle and brag in each, and think God can tell them apart at that distance and has nothing better to do than try. *This*—the entertainment of an eternity—...No, this is not blasphemy. (Blasphemy is the disrespectful remarks from you about my god. Irreverence is the lack of reverence for *my* sacred things on your part. But I don't have to respect *your* fetishes. [64]) If God is as vast as that, He is above blasphemy; if He is as little as that, He is beneath it." [65]

28

REGARDING Mark Twain's views toward Christian Science, about which there has been much discussion and varying opinions, he definitely approved of it as a mental science. In 1896, he wrote his daughter, Susy: ". . . Mamma is busy with my pen, declining invitations. And all because we haven't you here to argue some of our stupid foolishnesses out of us and replace them with healthy thoughts—and by consequence physical soundness. I caught cold last night. . .and am shut up in the hotel starving it out. . .It is too bad—yes, and too ridiculous. I am perfectly certain that the exasperating colds and the carbuncles came from a diseased mind, and that your mental science could drive them away, if we only had you here to properly apply it. . .how glad and grateful I am that you are a convert to that rational and noble philosophy. Stick to it; don't let anybody talk you out of it." [66]

By 1900, he said: "I cannot help feeling rather inordinately proud of America for the gay and hearty way in which she takes hold of any new thing that comes along and gives it a first rate trial. Many an ass is getting a deal of benefit out of Christian Science's new exploitation of an age-old healing principle—*faith*, combined with the patient's imagination—let it boom along!" [67]

One day in 1906, his biographer, Albert Bigelow Paine, confessed reluctantly that his own neurasthenia had been greatly benefitted by Christian Science. This occurred after the publication of Twain's articles on Christian Science, in which he had become known as its chief public antagonist. But the humorist surprised Paine by answering: "Of course you have been benefitted. Christian Science is humanity's boon. Mother Eddy deserves a place in the Trinity as much as any member of it. She has organized and made available a healing principle that for two thousand years has never been employed, except as the merest kind of guesswork. She is the benefactor of the age." [68]

Again, in 1907, he wrote an encouraging letter to his third daughter, Jean, who was afflicted with epilepsy:

"...in my heart I have no reproaches for you, but only mournings for your unearned estate.

"What I would like, for your best sake, would be for you to force your mind away from your self and concentrate it upon a trying but valuable task: the task of making some difficult person happy...The very best part of the Christian Science philosophy is that very thing: driving one's mind away from its own concerns and riveting it upon something else—and closely watching it and *keeping* it there. You can do this—we all can—and it brings healing to the spirit and is estimably valuable ..." [69]

In the same year he wrote a friend:

"Won't you please try Mr. Paine's 'Christian Scientist'? He ... helped some kind of ailment of Clara's ... and restored John Howells to good and sound health when he had long been a wreck and just a museum of pestilent maladies....Put aside prejudice—prejudice is nobody's sure friend." [69a]

Twain's criticism was of Mary Baker Eddy, since he had the impression she had attached a business to religion. Also he felt she was building up a powerful machine to eventually control America. As a writer he examined her literary style, compared her *Autobiography* and *Science and Health,* and claimed she could not possibly have been the author of both. But then, he had also believed that Bacon wrote Shakespeare's plays. This accounts for his calling Shakespeare and Mrs. Eddy "a pair of humbugs."

Eight months before his death he wrote:

"My view...has not changed. To-wit, that Christian Science is valuable, that it has just the same value now that it had when Mrs. Eddy [took] it from Quimby; that its healing principle (its most valuable asset) possesses the same force now that it possessed a million years before Quimby was born; that Mrs. Eddy...*organized* that force and is *entitled to high credit for that.* Then with a splendid sagacity she hitched it to the shirttail of a religion—the surest of all ways to secure friends for it, and support..." [70]

Twain noted inconsistencies and faults also in the Catholic Church, but he was equally ready to recognize its benefits. Although he grew up under Protestanism; was a member, however briefly in 1861, of the Masonic Lodge in St. Louis, and criticized the Roman Catholic

31

Church roundly in *The Innocents Abroad* and *A Connecticut Yankee*, he freed himself in time of the prejudices of anti-Catholics. In Europe he criticized the repetitious relics, some of the "miracles," and what he considered to be unjust activities of the Catholic priests, but where the Church touched him personally he was quick to praise it.

Again in an effort to find help for his ailing Jean, he agreed to have her put in a convent. Jean, then fifteen, stayed but a short time, but her father commented:

"I am very, very glad Jean is in a convent . . . Away down deep in my heart I feel that if they make a good strong unshakable Catholic of her I shan't be the least bit sorry. It is doubtless the most peace-giving and restful of all the religions. If I had it I would not trade it for anything in the earth. If I ever change my religion I shall change to that."[70a]

ANOTHER favorite topic for Twain was Providence:

"There is this trouble about special providences—namely, there is so often a doubt as to which party was intended to be the beneficiary. In the case of the children, the bears, and the prophet, the bears got more real satisfaction out of the episode than the prophet did, because they got the children." [71]

"We are accustomed to seeing the hand of Providence in everything. . . . When Providence washes one of his worms into the sea in a tempest, then starves him and freezes him on a plank for thirty-four days, and finally wrecks him again on an uninhabited island, where he lives on shrimps and grasshoppers for three months, and is at last rescued by some old whisky-soaked, profane. . . infidel of a tramp captain, and carried home gratis to his friends, the worm forgets that it was Providence that washed him overboard, and only remembers that Providence rescued him." [72]

The San Francisco fire in 1906, again reminded Twain of the ways of Providence. In lighter mood he observed that the building of the *Morning Call* newspaper had been destroyed forty years after its editor had discharged him as a reporter:

"Some people would think it curious that Providence should destroy an entire city of 400,000 inhabitants to settle an account of forty years' standing, between a mere discharged reporter and a newspaper, but to me there was nothing strange about that, because I was . . . trained, I was a Presbyterian, and I know how these things are done. I knew that in Biblical times, if a man committed a sin, the extermination of the whole surrounding nation— cattle and all—was likely to happen. I knew that Providence was not particular about the rest, so that He got somebody connected with the one He was after. I remembered that in the *Magnalia* a man who went home swearing from prayer meeting one night got his reminder within the next nine months. He had a wife and seven children, and all at once they were attacked by a terrible disease, and one by one they died . . . till at the end of a week there was nothing left but the man himself. I knew that the idea was to punish the man, and I knew that if he had any intelligence he recognized that that intention had been carried out, although mainly at the expense of other people." [73]

He added, in a letter: "I never count any prospective chickens when I know that Providence knows where the nest is." [74]

ONE OF Twain's strongest beliefs was in predeterminism: "I positively believe that the first circumstance that ever happened in this world was the parent of every circumstance that has happened in this world since; that God ordered that first circumstance and has never ordered another one from that day to this. Plainly, then, I am not able to conceive of such a thing as . . . an *accident*—that is to say, an event without a cause. Each event has its own place in the eternal chain of circumstances, and whether it be big or little it will infallibly cause the *next* event, whether the next event be the breaking of a child's toy or the destruction of a throne." [75]

Following this theory, he wrote: "Necessarily the scene of the real turning-point of my life (and of yours) was the Garden of Eden. It was there that the first link was forged of the chain that was ultimately to lead to the emptying of me into the literary guild. Adam's *temperament* was the first command the Deity ever issued to a human being on this planet. And it was the only command Adam would *never* be able to disobey. It said, 'Be weak, be water, be characterless, be cheaply persuadable.' The later command, to let the fruit alone, was certain to be disobeyed. Not by Adam himself, but by his *temperament*—which he did not create and had no authority over. For the *tem-*

35

perament is the man; the thing tricked out with clothes and named Man is merely its Shadow, nothing more . . .

"I cannot help feeling disappointed in Adam and Eve. That is, in their temperaments. Not in *them*, poor helpless young creatures—afflicted with temperaments made out of butter, which butter was commanded to get into contact with fire and be *melted*. What I cannot help wishing is, that Adam and Eve had been postponed, and Martin Luther and Joan of Arc put in their place—that splendid pair equipped with temperaments not made of butter, but of asbestos. By neither sugary persuasions nor by hell-fire could Satan have beguiled *them* to eat the apple.

"There would have been results! Indeed yes. The apple would be intact to-day; there would be no human race; there would be no *you*; there would be no *me*; And the old, old creation-dawn scheme of ultimately launching me into the literary guild would have been defeated." [76]

RETURNING to the Bible, to which we have seen Twain refer constantly: "The Christian's Bible is a drug store," he said. "Its contents remain the same; but the medical practice changes. During many ages there were witches.

The Bible said so. The Bible commanded that they should not be allowed to live. Therefore the Church, after doing its duty in but a lazy and indolent way for 800 years, gathered up its halters, thumbscrews, and firebrands, and set about its holy work in earnest. She worked hard at it night and day during nine centuries and imprisoned, tortured, hanged, and burned whole hordes and armies of witches, and washed the Christian world clean with their foul blood.

"Then it was discovered that there was no such thing as witches, and never had been. One does not know whether to laugh or to cry. Who discovered that there was no such thing as a witch—the priest, the parson? No, these never discover anything. At Salem, the parson clung pathetically to his witch text after the laity had abandoned it in remorse and tears for the crimes and cruelties it had persuaded them to do. The parson wanted more blood, more shame, more brutalities; it was the unconsecrated laity that stayed his hand . . .

"There are no witches. The witch text remains; only the practice has changed. Hell fire has gone, but the text remains. Infant damnation is gone, but the text remains . . . It does certainly seem to suggest that if man continue in the direction of enlightenment, his religious practice may, in the end, attain some semblance of human decency." [77]

AT the age of 61, Twain was still objecting to the Bible's presentation of God:

"If I were going to construct a God," he said, "I would furnish Him with some ways and qualities and characteristics which the present Bible One lacks.

"He would not stoop to *ask* for any man's compliments, praises, flatteries; and He would be far above *exacting* them. I would have Him as self-respecting as the better sort of man in these regards.

"He would not be a merchant, a trader. He would not buy these things. He would not sell, or offer to sell, temporary benefits or the joys of eternity for the product called worship. I would have Him as dignified as the better sort of men in this regard.

"He would value no love but the love born of kindnesses conferred; not that born of benevolences contracted for. Repentance in a man's heart for a wrong done would cancel and annul that sin, and no verbal prayers for forgiveness be required or desired or expected of that man.

"In His Bible there would be no Unforgivable Sin. He would recognize in Himself the Author and Inventor of Sin and Author and Inventor of the Vehicle and Appliances for its commission; and would place the whole responsibility where it would of right belong: upon Himself, the only Sinner.

38

"He would not be a jealous God—a trait so small that even men despise it in each other.

"He would not boast.

"He would keep private His admirations of Himself; He would regard self-praise as unbecoming the dignity of His position.

"He would not have the spirit of vengeance in His heart; then it would not issue from His lips.

"There would not be any hell—except the one we live in from the cradle to the grave.

"There would not be any heaven—of the kind described in the world's Bibles.

"He would spend some of His eternities in trying to forgive Himself for making man unhappy when He could have made him happy with the same effort and He would spend the rest of them in studying astronomy." [78]

Twain admired the serene assurance of those who have religious faith. He said; "It is wonderful to observe the calm confidence of a Christian with four aces." [79]

To all appearances the humorist had found what he believed to be the Truth. "Prayer alone," he said, "cannot change the unalterable Truth, or give us an understanding of it; but prayer coupled with a fervent habitual desire to know and do the will of God will bring us into all Truth. Such a desire has little need of audible expression. It is best expressed in thought and life." [80]

Prayers for rain or for individual needs shocked Twain. The implications of personal petitions are illustrated in

39

his powerful "War Prayer," which seems to be continuously appropriate:

"O Lord our Father, our young patriots, idols of our hearts, go forth to battle—be Thou near them! With them—in spirit—we also go forth from the sweet peace of our beloved firesides to smite the foe. O Lord our God, help us to tear their soldiers to bloody shreds with our shells; help us to cover their smiling fields with the pale forms of their patriot dead; help us to drown the thunder of the guns with the shrieks of their wounded, writhing in pain; help us to lay waste their humble homes with a hurricane of fire; help us to wring the hearts of their unoffending widows with unavailing grief; help us to turn them out roofless with their little children to wander unfriended the wastes of their desolated land in rags and hunger and thirst, sports of the sun flames of summer and the icy winds of winter, broken in spirit, worn with travail, imploring Thee for the refuge of the grave and denied it—for our sakes who adore Thee, Lord, blast their hopes, blight their lives, protract their bitter pilgrimage, make heavy their steps, water their way with their tears, stain the white snow with the blood of their wounded feet! We ask it, in the spirit of love, of Him Who is the Source of Love, and Who is the ever-faithful refuge and friend of all that are sore beset and seek His aid with humble and contrite hearts.   Amen."

He believed himself to be satisfied as a doubter. After he had called onthe widow of the explorer Henry Stanley, and found her to be an intense spiritualist, Twain wrote:

"...To me, who take no interest in other-worldly things and am convinced that we know nothing whatever about them and have been wrongly and uncourteously and contemptuously left in total ignorance of them, it is a pleasure and a refreshment to have converse with a person like Lady Stanley, who uncompromisingly believes in them...She was as exactly and as comprehensively happy and content in her beliefs as I am in my destitution of them, and I perceived that we could exchange places and both of us be precisely as well off as we were before; for when all is said and done, the one sole condition that makes spiritual happiness and preserves it is the absence of doubt...Lady Stanley wanted to convert me to her beliefs and her faith, and there has been a time when I would have been eager to convert her to my position, but that time has gone by; I would not now try to unsettle any person's religious faith, where it was untroubled by doubt..."[81]

But he was back "at it" again in 1898, writing in his notebook his own ideas of God:

"The Being who to me is the real God is the One who created this majestic universe and rules it. He is the only Originator, the only originator of thoughts, thoughts suggested from within not from without; the originator of colors and of all their possible combinations; of forces and the laws that govern them; of forms and shapes of *all* forms. Man has never invented a new one; He is the only

41

Originator—He made the materials of all things; He made the laws by which, and by which only, many may combine them into machines and other things which outside influence may suggest to Him. He made character—man can portray it but not 'create' it, for He is the only Creator.

"He is the perfect artisan, the perfect artist. Every thing which He has made is fine, everything which He has made is beautiful: nothing coarse, nothing ugly has ever come from His hand. Even His materials are all delicate, none of them is coarse. The materials of the leaf, the flower, the fruit; of the insect, the elephant, the man; of the earth, the crags and the ocean; of the snow, the hoarfrost and the ice—may be reduced to infinitesimal particles and they are still delicate, still faultless; whether He makes a gnat, a bird, a horse, a plain, a forest, a mountain range, a planet, a constellation, or a diatom whose form the keenest eye in the world cannot perceive, it is all one—He makes utterly and minutely perfect in form, and construction. The diatom which is invisible to the eye on the point of a needle is graceful and beautiful in form and in the minute exquisite elaboration of its parts it is a wonder. The contemplation of it moves one to something of the same awe and reverence which the march of the comets through their billion mile orbits compels.

"This is indeed a God! He is not jealous, trivial, ignorant, revengeful—it is impossible. He has personal dignity—dignity answerable to His grandeur, His greatness, His might, His sublimity; He cares nothing for men's praises and prayers; it is impossible that He should value them, impossible that He should listen to them, these mouthings of microbes. He is not ignorant, He does not mistake His myriad great suns, swimming in the measureless ocean of space for tallow candles hung in the roof to light this forgotten potato which we call the Earth, and name His footstool. He cannot see it except under His microscope. The shadow does not go back on His dial— it is against His law; His sun does not stand still on Gibeon to accommodate a worm out on a raid against other worms—it is against His law. His real character is written in plain words in His real Bible, which is Nature and her history; we read it every day, and we could understand it and trust in it if we would burn the spurious one and dig the remains of our insignificant reasoning faculties out of the grave where that and other man-made Bibles have buried them for 2000 years and more.

"The Bible of Nature tells us no word about any future life, but only about this present one. [Is there any Word of God except geology, paleontology and astronomy? [82]] The Bible of Nature does not promise a future life: it does not even vaguely indicate one. It is not intended as a message to us, any more than the scientist intends a message to surviving microbes when he boils the life out of a billion of them in a thimble. The microbes discover a message in it; this is certain—if they have a pulpit.

"The Book of Nature tells us distinctly that God cares not a rap for us—nor for any living creature. It tells us it does not say that this is done in order that He may get pleasure out of this misery. We do not know what the object is, for the Book is not able to tell us. It may be mere indifference. Without a doubt He had an object, but we have no way of discovering what it was. The scientist has an object, but it is not the joy of inflicting pain upon the microbe.

"The Law of Distribution of Comfort and Pain shows an entire absence of sentimental justice. The proportion of punishments to the size of the infractions has been ignored; this again shows the absence of anything representing sentimental justice." [83]

Finally, in his later life, Twain recorded certain conclusions from which he did not deviate thereafter:

"I believe in God Almighty.

"I do not believe He has ever sent a message to man by anybody, or delivered one to him by word of mouth, or made Himself visible to mortal eyes at any time in any place.

"I believe that the Old and New Testaments were imagined and written by man, and that no line in them was authorized by God, much less inspired by Him.

"I think the goodness, the justice, and the mercy of God are manifested in His works: I perceive that they are manifested toward me in this life; the logical conclusion is that they will be manifested toward me in the life to come, if there should be one.

"I do not believe in special providences. I believe that the universe is governed by strict and immutable laws. If one man's family is swept away by a pestilence and another man's spared it is only the law working: God is not interfering in that small matter, either against the one man or in favor of the other.

"I cannot see how eternal punishment hereafter could accomplish any good end, therefore I am not able to believe in it. To chasten a man in order to perfect him might be reasonable enough; to annihilate him when he shall have proved himself incapable of reaching perfection might be reasonable enough; but to roast him forever for the mere satisfaction of seeing him roast would not be reasonable—even the atrocious God imagined by the Jews would tire of the spectacle eventually.

"There may be a hereafter and there may *not* be. I am wholly indifferent about it. If I am appointed to live again I feel sure it will be for some more sane and useful purpose than to flounder about for ages in a lake of fire and brimstone for having violated a confusion of ill-defined and contradictory rules said (but not evidenced) to be of divine institution. If annihilation is to follow death I shall not be aware of the annihilation, and therefore shall not care a straw about it.

"I believe that the world's moral laws are the outcome of the world's experience. It needed no God to come down out of heaven to tell men that murder and theft and the other immoralities were bad, both for the individual who commits them and for society which suffers from them.

"If I break all these moral laws I cannot see how I injure God by it, for He is beyond the reach of injury from me—I could as easily injure a planet by throwing mud at it. It seems to me that my misconduct could only injure me and other men. I cannot benefit God by obeying these moral laws—I could as easily benefit the planet by withholding my mud. (Let these sentences be read in the light of the fact that I believe I have received moral laws *only* from man—none whatever from God.) Consequently I do not see why I should be either punished or rewarded hereafter for the deeds I do here." [84]

Whether he was right or wrong, Twain had the integrity to say what he believed, though he was tempted often to be facetious. Once, when asked whether he believed in the existence of heaven or hell, he replied: "I don't want to express an opinion. I have friends in both places."

It was characteristic of him to offer solace to those who did not believe as he believed:

"The easy confidence with which I know another man's religion is folly teaches me to suspect that my own is also."

He added: "I would not interfere with any one's religion, either to strengthen it or to weaken it...It may easily be a great comfort to him—hence it is a valuable possession to him." [85]

On one subject—that of immortality—Mark Twain appeared to vacillate, yet he may have done this to spare the feelings of those dear to him. In his notebook he had written: "One of the proofs of the immortality of the soul is that myriads have believed in it. They also believed the world was flat."[86]

Later: "As to the hereafter, we have not the slightest evidence that there is any—*no* evidence that appeals to logic and reason. I have never seen what to me seemed an atom of proof that there is a future life." But, he added: "And yet—I am strongly inclined to expect one."[87]

After he saw that he had grieved his wife by his denial of immortality, he resolved upon an heroic lie, which for love's sake he held above even the truth. According to Howells, Twain went to Livy, "saying he had been thinking the whole matter over, and now he was convinced that the soul did live after death. It was too late. Her keen vision pierced through his ruse..."[88]

Still later, in a letter, he wrote:

"Livy darling, it broke my heart—what you wrote... about immortality. Let us believe in it! I will believe in it with you. It had been the belief of the wise and thoughtful of many countries for three thousand years; let us accept their verdict; we cannot frame one that is more reasonable or probable. I will try never to doubt it again."[89]

And this was the man whose last words to his daughter, Clara, were:

"Goodbye dear, if we meet—"

Reference Notes

1 *Mark Twain At Your Fingertips*, p. 456
2 Marginal note in *Views of Religion*, unpublished
3 *Mark Twain's Notebook*, p. 153
4 Marginal note, *Views of Religion*
5 *A Tramp Abroad*, I, p. 230
6 *Notebook*, p. 344
7 *Mark Twain, a Biography*, II, p. 631
8 *Ibid*, p. 776
9 *Notebook*, p. 108
10 *Biography*, III, p. 1313
11 *Mark Twain-Howells Letters*, II, p. 461
12 *Mark Twain's Autobiography*, I, p. 131
13 *Huckleberry Finn*, p. 200
14 *A Connecticut Yankee*, p. 146
15 *Mark Twain's Speeches* (1923), p. 251
16 Marginal note, *Views of Religion*
17 *Mark Twain, Family Man*, p. 83
18 Marginal note, *Views of Religion*
19 *Autobiography*, II, p. 13
20 "Concerning the Jews," *Literary Essays*, p. 251
21 *Sam Clemens of Hannibal*, p. 228
22 *Ibid*, p. 231
23 *Mark Twain's Travels with Mr. Brown*, p. 146
24 *Notebook*, p. 310
25 Marginal note, *Views of Religion*
26 *The Innocents Abroad*, II, p. 245
26a *Autobiography*. II, p. 15
27 Marginal note, *Views of Religion*
28 *Biography*, I, p. 411
29 Letter, Jan. 2, 1869, *Mark Twain, Family Man*, p. 58
30 *My Mark Twain*, p. 31

[31] Letter to Caroline Thomas Harnsberger, August 20, 1960, unpublished
[32] *Biography*, II, p. 165
[33] *Love Letters of Mark Twain*, p. 167 (Jan. 7, 1872)
[34] Letter, Olivia Clemens to Samuel Clemens, Jan. 7, 1872, unpublished
[35] Isabelle Lyon re Twain's gospel. Berg collection, New York Public Library
[36] Letter, May 20, 1905, *Mark Twain, Family Man*, p. 217
[37] *Biography*, II, p. 631
[38] Edward Wagenknecht, letter to Caroline Thomas Harnsberger, Aug. 2, 1960, unpublished
[39] *Biography*, I, p. 412
[40] Marginal note, *Views of Religion*
[41] *Ibid*
[42] *Ibid*
[43] *Ibid*
[44] *Mark Twain's Letters*, I, p. 323
[44a] *Mark Twain, the Man and His Work*, p.191
[45] *Mark Twain in Eruption*, p. 50
[45a] Marginal Note, *Views of Religion*
[46] *Europe and Elsewhere*, p. 249
[47] Marginal Note, *Views of Religion*
[48] *Notebook*, p. 21
[49] *Roughing It*, II, p. 216
[50] *Mark Twain's Speeches* (1910) p. 117
[51] *Notebook*, p. 397
[52] *Biography*, III, p. 1354
[53] Marginal note, *Views of Religion*
[54] *More Maxims of Mark*, p. 8
[55] "Concerning the Jews," *Literary Essays*, p. 274
[56] *Biography*, III, p. 1355
[57] Unpublished notebook, June 20, 1906
[58] Marginal note, *Views of Religion*

[59] *Mark Twain At Your Fingertips*, p. 492
[60] *Sketches of Creation*, p. 160, 162, unpublished notes
[61] *Ibid*, inside cover, and p. 431
[62] *Ibid*, p. 313
[63] *Ibid*, p. 427
[64] Marginal note, *Views of Religion*
[65] *Biography*, III, p. 1354
[66] *Love Letters*, p. 316 (Feb. 7, 1896)
[67] *Mark Twain Letters*, II, p. 690
[68] *Biography*, III, p. 1271 (1906)
[69] *Mark Twain, Family Man*, p. 232
[69a] *Mark Twain's Letters to Mary*, p. 107
[70] *The Portable Mark Twain*, p. 786 (Aug. 7, 1909)
[70a] *My Father Mark Twain*, p. 100
[71] *Puddn'head Wilson*, p. 38
[72] *Autobiography*, I, p. 209
[73] *Mark Twain in Eruption*, p. 260
[74] *Mark Twain-Howells Letters*, I, p. 445
[75] *Mark Twain in Eruption*, p. 386
[76] *Biography*, III, p. 1545
[77] "Bible Teaching & Religious Practice," *Europe and Elsewhere*, p. 387
[78] *Notebook*, p. 301
[79] *The Washoe Giant in San Francisco*, p. 62
[80] *Christian Science*, p. 321
[80a] *Europe and Elsewhere*, p. 397
[81] *Mark Twain in Eruption*, p. 339
[82] Marginal note, *Views of Religion*
[83] *Notebook*, p. 360
[84] *Biography*, III, p. 1583
[85] *Ibid*, p. 1584
[86] *Notebook*, p. 344
[87] *Biography*, III, p. 1431
[88] *My Mark Twain*, p. 32
[89] *My Father, Mark Twain*, p. 177

Bibliography

Clemens, Clara. *My Father, Mark Twain.* New York: Harper & Brothers, 1931.

———An unpublished letter.

Clemens, Olivia. An unpublished letter.

De Voto, Bernard. *Mark Twain in Eruption.* New York: Harper & Brothers, 1940.

——— *The Portable Mark Twain.* New York: The Viking Press, 1946.

Harnsberger, Caroline Thomas. *Mark Twain at Your Fingertips.* New York: Beechhurst Press, 1948.

——— *Mark Twain, Family Man.* New York: The Citadel Press, 1960.

Howells, William Dean. *My Mark Twain.* New York: Harper & Brothers, 1910.

Leary, Lewis. *Mark Twain's Letters to Mary.* New York: Columbia University Press, 1961.

Noyes, Rufus K. *Views of Religion,* with previously unpublished marginal notes by Mark Twain. Boston: L. K. Washburn, 1906.

Paine, Albert Bigelow. *Mark Twain's Autobiography.* New York: Harper & Brothers, 1924.

——— *Mark Twain, a Biography.* 3 vols. New York: Harper & Brothers, 1912.

——— *Mark Twain's Letters.* 2 vols. New York: Harper & Brothers, 1917.

——— Mark Twain's Notebook. New York: Harper & Brothers, 1935.

Smith, Henry Nash and William M. Gibson. *Mark Twain-Howells Letters*. Cambridge: Harvard University Press, 1960.

Twain, Mark. *Christian Science*. New York: Harper & Brothers, 1899.

——— *A Connecticut Yankee*. New York: Harper & Brothers, 1899·

——— *Europe and Elsewhere*. New York: Harper & Brothers, 1923.

——— *Huckleberry Finn*. New York: Harper & Brothers, 1899.

——— *The Innocents Abroad*. New York: Harper & Brothers, 1899.

——— *Literary Essays*. New York: Harper & Brothers, 1899.

——— *More Maxims of Mark*. New York: Privately printed. 1927.

——— *Puddn'head Wilson*. New York: Harper & Brothers, 1899.

——— *Roughing It*. New York: Harper & B6others, 1899.

——— *Speeches*. New York: Harper & Brothers, 1910.

——— *A Tramp Abroad*. New York: Harper & Brothers, 1899.

Wagenknecht, Edward. *Mark Twain, the Man and His Work*. Oklahoma City: Oklahoma University Press, 1961.

Walker, Franklin. *The Washoe Giant in San Francisco*. San Francisco: George Fields, 1938.

——— and G. Ezra Dane. *Mark Twain's Travels with Mr. Brown*. New York: Alfred A. Knopf, 1940.

Wecter, Dixon. *The Love Letters of Mark Twain*. New York: Harper & Brothers, 1949.

Winchell, Alexander, LL.D. *Sketches of Creation*, with marginal notes by Mark Twain. New York: Harper & Brothers, 1903.

 *the schori press*

THIS BOOK in all its phases, including
design and artwork, is the result
of the close cooperation
between author and printer-publisher.

Printing is from Baskerville type on Strathmore
Text 400 copies, Strathmore Pastelle 100
copies, all numbered. Twenty-six additional
copies lettered A to Z on Imported Swedish
Hand-Made paper. This is Copy *364.*

Ward K. Schori